D1003023

The Blue Vase

Go-Getters Come in All Ages

Andree Marie Ory

WESTBOW
PRESS®
A DIVISION OF THOMAS NELSON
& ZONDERVAN

WestBow Press books may be ordered through booksellers or by contacting:

WestBow Press
A Division of Thomas Nelson & Zondervan
1663 Liberty Drive
Bloomington, IN 47403
www.westbowpress.com
1 (866) 928-1240

ISBN: 978-1-5127-7933-2 (sc)
ISBN: 978-1-5127-7934-9 (e)

Print information available on the last page.

WestBow Press rev. date: 04/26/2017

DEDICATION PAGE

To My Dad, who passed down to me his passionate temperament and who vicariously, spontaneously, verbally, and intentionally showed me who I was, reminded me of who I could become, and whose most important words to me recently were: "I'm proud of you."

To God: who leads me into unknown, uncharted waters compelled by the strongest force in the universe. He is the only one capable of calling me and challenging me: changing a soul like mine into my best, loving, tender, creative, compassionate and self. He enhances and ennobles my inherent desire for both Him and for greatness in both human endeavors and in moral excellence. He reveals my weaknesses to me; loving me through them, in spite of them, and even more: because of them.

To Theresa Schopler, who encouraged me to "go for it," and write this book. After all, as she said, "Why not? You're young."

Contents

From a young age, I began imitating my dad.

You're never too old for a dad/daughter
birthday dinner date. #27

AIRPORT MEETING AND BLUE VASES

Background: October 28, 2016. My dad and I are in the New Orleans airport on the way to see a Notre Dame game. I have just moved to a different town, and I missed my dad. So I made up an excuse for us to spend time together and played the "Dad, I missed out card." You see, he took the four youngest (minus me) in my family to see the Fighting Irish play football. I was the only one that politely declined because I was always studying or busy with high school or college activities. Going away to a freezing cold place to see a sport I didn't love in the middle of a huge work-week (homework wise in high school, college, and grad school) was not my cup of tea back then.

Present: As my dad and I are nearing the gate, I see him looking out for people he knows. Of course he would. That's my dad. A dentist by trade and a historian and farmer by hobby, he loves people and is passionate about them. One of the reasons he became a dentist is because he loved seeing how his father and grandfather before him were well-known in the community and knew everyone. My dad is a servant leader by nature, as intense as they come. This intense profession fit him perfectly.

Before I have time to wonder why my dad is craning his head to look for someone, I see a couple in the airport. My dad breathlessly says something about "one of his old dental school buddies" and "the couple Mom and I went out with last night" being at our same gate and going to the same destination before I get to meet the complete strangers. This is soooo typical of my dad. It's 5 in the morning, and I'm not happy. Who would without coffee at 4:30 in the morning? Even for something as exciting as a football game!

About ten minutes later, the wife introduces herself to me as Theresa. Before you know it, we are talking like old friends and an instant connection was made. Little did I know that we would begin to FaceBook message each other almost every day and that she would play a major role in my writing.

"Oh, so what do you do?" was her question that started it all. "Well, I just started my own business as a skincare consultant; I substitute at a nursery, and I sit three nights a week for this elderly lady. Oh, and I write for my own Catholic blog and personal website," was my long and detailed reply. After chit-chatting about the skincare products we use in common and how they have helped our skin look so much better, she said, "I loved your articles you wrote while you were counseling. Tell me about the Blue Vase again." After explaining to her the idea behind my blog about go-getters in each phase of Erikson's stages of psychosocial development, she candidly replied, "Well, that's what you need to do. That's your gift. You need to write."

I liked to write before and knew I had some talent but did not truly see it as my gift. Yes, I already had two book ideas inside of me and future writing projects, but no, I did not think that I was particularly gifted in this area. It was more of something that God inspired me to do and I followed one step at a time (on the side, while pursuing a career in the world of babies and in skincare).

Fast forward: Today's date is December 3rd. As promised, this book is dedicated to Theresa Schopler, who stayed in touch with me and sent me pictures throughout the weekend. Yes, Notre Dame won. We played Miami. No, I don't remember much about the game. Yes, we had a charmed trip with much needed and cherished father/daughter time.

A Keepsake from our Dad/Daughter Notre Dame Trip

"Work hard. Play hard. Go get 'em, Dree." –My Dad

This series of stores is dedicated to my father, an example of a classic go-getter who suggested I read this book in the first place.

"What is the blue vase?" asks author Peter Kyne towards the end of The Go-Getter, his classic, inspirational parable about one man's near impossible quest to secure a blue vase his boss demands to prove his resourcefulness and loyalty. Just as Bill Peck, the hero of the story, has to face his fears, his weaknesses, his insecurities, and inconvenient life circumstances in order to prevail, we also face obstacles like this one every day.

We may not be a war veteran with an amputated arm and an injured leg, like Bill. We may not have a boss devising quests to see if we prove worthy of a lucrative job in Shanghai, as Bill did. We may not have to chase down a reluctant store manager on a Sunday afternoon, as Bill did.

But we're only fooling ourselves if we read these lines, shake our heads, and say: "Not me. I don't have a blue vase."

Look again.

"Life is hard, Andree," my mom told me once over the phone in a poignant conversation. "My generation a Mimi's generation always knew that. Your generatio kids today are surprised by this." For those 15 and Generation Z, their first blue vase is the shock dose of reality slapping them in the face. Life can be plagued with many questions. Why get divorced? Why am I failing two subje am I being bullied? For many memb

Generation Y, the questions are different. Why didn't I get that job? Why didn't that relationship work out? Why do I have so many loans to pay off? For generations a little bit older, Generation X, the blue vase might look a little different. Why didn't I get that promotion? Why did my wife leave me? Why don't I ever get enough sleep? Why don't I ever have enough time? For baby boomers, the blue vase might be: Why didn't I save up for retirement when I had the chance? Why don't my kids come to visit? Why did that good person get cancer? For Traditionals, the blue vase could be: Why don't I remember like I used to? Why do I feel so tired all the time? Why am I so lonely? Why won't my body keep up with my mind? You get the picture.

Since we all have blue vases, how do we overcome our fears, limitations and difficult life circumstances? In addition to practicing the virtues of courage, persistence, loyalty, and determination, like Peter Kyne suggests, here are a few tips from psychologist Albert Bandura.

⸱ɔ Bandura, in order for us to boost our self-
ɔnfidence in our competency in a certain
⸱ things:

⸱t grand slams and remind ourselves
ʌ.

ɔur role models.

milies, and mentors for

4) Look inside ourselves and pay attention to what our bodies are telling us.

The first three are self-explanatory. The last one refers to what counselors call mindfulness: paying attention to your physiological responses to see what your body is telling you about a given situation. Slow down long enough to let those butterflies calm down, which allows one to think clearly and rationally resolve the situation.

Sometimes, you don't know what your blue vase is; other times, you know what it is but may be paralyzed by fear. Counselors are here to help you identify your blue vase and help stir up your inner go-getter to develop a smart strategy to not just locate that blue vase but to chase that one down and identify and go for many others as well.

Go-getters don't just read about success. They are men and women of action. Now get up and go get it!

"Grit is passion and perseverance for very long term goals. Grit is having stamina. Grit is sticking with your future: day in, day out—not just for the week, not just for the month, but for years, and working very hard to make that future a reality. Grit is living life like it's a marathon, not a sprint."

Angela Lee Duckworth

Ryan is "stubborn, persistent, has a big heart, and does not let go very easily of questions," reports Paul, his dad.

This is good news.

According to Dr. Angela Lee Duckworth, persistence and patience in the pursuit of excellence are indicators of success in the future. She calls this passion and perseverance for very long term goals "grit," and Ryan shows early signs of it.

He is forging the beginnings of a personality trait and establishing a firm sense of identity and self-confidence that will buttress his competency as an adult.

Our twelve-year-old go-getter for this month is cultivating a growing confidence in his own capabilities. Children from 5-11 typically are striving to succeed in school, making friends, and engaging sports, hobbies, etc., according to Erikson. If, for whatever reason, those tasks do not go well, a child may be at risk for developing a sense of inadequacy in responding to the challenges of life.

Measuring something as subjective as self-confidence in any certain area is not easy. Nevertheless, I took a shot at it by asking Ryan scaling questions like:

"On a scale of 1-10, how likely do you think you could accomplish your dream of being a cosmologist, a salesman, an engineer, or a doctor?"

He gave himself a 10. He firmly replied, "As long as you work hard, you can do it. You're in America."

"Ryan, are you sure you understand the question? How much do you believe that you could achieve the minimum requirements necessary to become a cosmologist, salesman, engineer, or a doctor? I'm asking you to give me a number between one and ten."

"Ten" was his firm and final answer.

With the exception of a career as a salesman, a common thread of science ran through his career choices. Watching History Channel videos on the universe with his dad is a favorite pastime. He and his dad share a love of science, so conversations about the "big questions of the universe" are normal. According to his dad, Ryan will research the answer to a question he doesn't know, rather than guessing at or inventing one. From a psychological perspective, this patience in the quest for truth is proof that this kid's got grit.

Here is further proof. When he is not as motivated, he goes to: God, then his parents, then his friends… "or I just Google the answer. Like if I'm upset, I'll Google it. You'd be surprised the answers you can come up with on the internet."

If Ryan continues to take his questions seriously, and to look, and look, and look until he finds the answer, I'd say his future looks pretty bright.

"T' WAS the best of times, it was the worst of times, it was the age of wisdom, it was the age of foolishness… it was the season of Light, it was the season of Darkness, it was the spring of hope, it was the winter of despair, we had everything before us, we had nothing before us…"

-Charles Dickens…A Tale of Two Cities

If I did not know any better, I would think that Dickens was talking about my high school experience rather than the French Revolution. Come to think of it, it's like he read the diaries of Gen Z high school kids too.

According to Erik Erikson, during the particularly trying and adventurous time we call adolescence (ages 12 to 18), teens undergo the stage of development called Identity vs. Confusion. The main virtue that they are striving to cultivate during this period is fidelity, by society's expectations and standards.

Our seventeen-year-old go-getter is a rebel in the sense that he shoots for the stars and does not let anyone's opinion block him from his goal. At the same time, he respects his parents and has a plan to stay within the bounds of their expectations as well as society's. Music has been his passion since the fourth grade, and he aims to make a career out of it instead of something more financially stable. You see, being at the top of his class in honors courses, he is not short of prestigious career options, medical school being one of them. He will make teaching music his main source of income while composing and playing on the side.

When asked how he feels about playing his particular instrument, he admitted that there are trials. "High notes are hard for me. It's hard to work for something I can't get instantly or easy. It's hard to accept defeat. I've always been first chair with music." He said that the only answer is to just keep practicing, whether someone is better than him or not.

He likes to stay quiet and "to organize things mentally and think through the best route to solving problems." One way he prioritized was choosing music over soccer at some point in high school. He credits God as a source of "comfort, inspiration, confidence, and energy" to do what has to be done and to "push through" when things are tough. He considers focusing more on his relationship with God, as he starts "missing who I was" in 7th-9th grade when he was active in church activities.

To over-come his perfectionism, he plays "mental games" with himself to keep himself in check and prioritize. "I think about what I've done, what I want to do, where I've been, and where I want to go." This "faithful rebel" knows his game plan and can sum it up in an eloquent way that Dickens might agree.

"In this world you've just got to hope for the best and prepare for the worst and take whatever God sends." L. M. Montgomery

September's Go-Getter

"I was able to push through…if there is something that I absolutely need to do, I'm gonna push through."

Meet Amy, a real go-getter. After being diagnosed with epilepsy as a teenager eleven years ago, this young professional working in media continues to push through – as when she filmed two major interviews on the same day after recovering from a seizure at work. She is currently going on her fourth year in her career, and this latest episode happened less than a year ago. She does not get embarrassed when an episode occurs in front of others. "It's just something that happens."

According to Erik Erikson, adolescents must pass through a psychosocial stage of development in which they establish a firm sense of self before, as young adults (like Amy and my generation, Gen Y) they can seek intimacy with others. Amy's firm sense of identity is evident in her statement: "Yeah, I have to deal with this. . . It's a fact of life . . . just an obstacle that I sometimes have." Because she has a firm sense of identity and has accepted that the reality of her situation requires her to take special care of herself, Amy can allow herself to be supported and loved by her family, boyfriend, and co-workers.

Amy's relationships have helped her to consider her epilepsy merely as a "small sacrifice" that requires her to take her medicine twice a day, exercise regularly, get at least seven hours of sleep a night, and steer clear of alcohol. Her dad helps her to remain positive, and her mom keeps her updated on all the possible triggers of epilepsy. Her family makes sure she has groceries once a week and drives her to events she is covering for work (typically three times a week). Her sister also "drops everything" for her if she needs it. Finally, she has been able to maintain a significant relationship with her boyfriend. She also is grateful to God, who protected her from oncoming traffic once when her car slid across the neutral ground after one particular episode.

John Bowlby and Mary Ainsworth are two researchers who highlighted four truths of secure relationships.

1) Loneliness can cause significant distress.

2) Connecting with others helps us to better manage our emotions.

3) We depend on others to answer our cries for help when we need it.

4) Experiencing the love and support of others helps us to become independent, confident people.

Amy has not only experienced the love of others who have helped her to become more secure, but she has formed solidarity with others who suffer. She reminds herself that others have epilepsy, and some suffer more than she. Still others have "lost loved ones" or have had other such "terrible situations" to overcome. Referring to her epilepsy, she says: "It challenges me to be grateful . . . and to know that it doesn't compromise my quality of life with the exception of driving. But I'm able to overcome that with the support of family and friends and my boyfriend." This solidarity with others is reflected in her attitude of gratitude and awareness of others who suffer.

In my last blog, I spoke of a fictional baby boomer who chased his blue vase – a quest imposed on him in pursuit of a job. After reading about Amy, a real-life go-getter, I challenge my generation especially to go deeper in their relationships with others – by reaching within themselves to build a strong sense of identity, and then reaching out to others.

Reach in. Reach out.

"The whole pleasure of marriage is that it is a perpetual crisis." GK Chesterton

John, a 35-year-old businessman, husband of ten years, and father of five, is our go-getter for this October issue. According to Erik Erikson, adults around the ages of 40-65 typically experience tension between balancing their careers and their personal lives. In John's case, he has decided to see himself primarily as a husband and a father. So he balances the tension by contributing to society and leaving a lasting legacy in and through his family first, and secondarily through his career or outside activities. In *Daring Greatly: How the Courage to Be Vulnerable Transforms the Way We Live, Love, Parent, and Lead*, social worker Brené Brown highlights eight characteristics of engaged, vulnerable, and courageous parenting – what she calls "wholehearted" parenting.

The first four involve teaching kids:

1) their intrinsic value.

2) to accept their flaws and limitations.

3) to live by the Golden rule.

4) to have a go-getter attitude and work ethic.

John definitely knows what it means to understand his own intrinsic value and to accept his flaws and limitations. John believes that "self-worth is not dependent on other people… it comes from God. If someone is critical, we should be humble enough to think criticism is deserved; we should not fear that."

Even though he used to be "fiercely independent," he and his fiancé (now his wife), went to pre-marital counseling at the urging of the priest after they had scored low on a compatibility test. He and his wife's work ethic is evident in their constant conversations about current family goals and how well they are meeting them. They adjust as they go, occasionally dropping extracurricular activities that take away one-on-one time from the kids. With role models such as Mother Teresa and Pope Francis, John is motivated to "help the poor and suffering," teaching his kids "joy and forgiveness." Concretely, he and his wife translate this compassion with their family by running 5ks together and going to galas as a family or as a couple.

The last four of Brown's characteristics of wholehearted parenting are to allow children to:

1) be genuine.

2) be open and innovative.

3) be confident during difficulties.

4) be brave and bounce back.

From his father, John learned to be kind while retaining one's integrity, and to stand for what he believed in, a lesson that he can pass on to his kids by spending one-on-one time with them so they can learn how he thinks, reacts, etc. They will learn to be open and innovative, learning from their mom and dad's wisdom and life experiences.

With regard to resiliency and being brave, John believes their household provides a "controlled laboratory to learn from these experiences in a more safe environment…before they are 13, 14, 15, without inner strength and coping mechanisms…" Rather than enabling kids that struggle emotionally, physically, intellectually, etc., he teaches them how to balance the tension between trying hard and accepting defeat. Also, when one child is struggling, he and his wife make a game plan to solve the issue rather than blaming the child or each other for the difficulty. Naturally, a child who is not blamed for physical, intellectual, or emotional struggles will be more confident in his or her ability to overcome and bounce back, relying on parents' unconditional love.

John and his wife's ultimate hope is that all of these things together lead "to emotionally mature adulthood, in which their children can engage the world on their own, and be happy, joyful, courageous individuals."

"There are dark shadows on the earth, but its lights are stronger in the contrast...The pain of parting is nothing compared to the joy of meeting again." Charles Dickens

As the year draws to a close and everyone is spreading holiday cheer, some of the older folks among us may be joining in the glee – or may not be feeling quite so cheerful. Some may dread facing another year of a difficult life, while others may feel like celebrating another year of new beginnings and opportunities. This annual review of life and past decisions is typical for people in the late autumn and winter of life, according to Erikson. They either feel integrity or despair – integrity in this case defined as facing the truth of who one is, accepting it, and reflecting that truth back to the world.

Viktor Frankl's *Man's Search for Meaning* may be especially helpful to those of this elder generation looking back at life and trying to make peace with past choices.

Frankl, a survivor of the Nazi death camp at Auschwitz, offers three insights for finding meaning in life.

1) Choose not to disappoint a loved one or God, who expects you to "suffer proudly—not miserably."

2) Love. Love. Love. That is "the highest goal."

3) Recognize your unique and irreplaceable responsibility for an "unfinished work."

Alice, our go-getter of December, demonstrates how to grow old gracefully. She "suffers proudly" for God first and her family second. She knows something of death already, having in middle age survived an operation that might have killed her; having experienced the grief of a young son's death, and served as her husband's sole caretaker during the last three years of his terminal illness. On her trips to and from the hospital and while caring for him at home, she helped relieve his anxiety about death by having him talk to their religious leader and researching his questions about the after-life.

Because addiction is present in her family, Alice has learned first-hand that love can be complicated and that it can be gentle or tough. Having to interact with those with addictions, she has learned the hard way how to exhibit tough love, demanding that others take responsibility for their lives. Although she has experienced guilt for past mistakes, she loves herself enough to "let go and live for today. Who knows if I'll be here tomorrow?"

Finally, her "unfinished work" has been to socialize with those her age who have experienced grief and to help them work past it. According to Alice, "That was one of the best things I've ever done. That's what saved me."

It takes courage to accept our past mistakes and share our true self to the world. May we all grow older gracefully and with dignity, finding someone or something to live for, someone to love, and a talent that we can share.

Afterword

Correspondence between Theresa and Andree

Andree: I just signed the deal with a publishing company for the Blue Vase! I'm working on the manuscript. I'm trying to figure out if I should include our story of the airport meeting in the afterword. I have it written. What do you think? Or just your blue vase picture with your message about how you have a blue vase too? And how we all do? Thoughts?

Theresa: Sure. Why not? It adds mystery, fate, life, intrigue. The blue vase was from my mother-in-law. Clara. She always had that blue vase on a shelf in her bedroom.

My husband and I faithfully included her in everything until she died at age 96. So I inherited that blue vase.

You know, we all have our blue vases. I also have a gorgeous small real Czech vase from my husband when we visited there last year.

If we go to (Theresa's hometown) I will send you the photo of the blue Bohemian Vase from Prague. It's the only authentic one in one store in Prague...Bohemian gypsy crystal."

Appendix

Bandura, Albert. (1977). Self-efficacy: Toward a unifying theory of behavioral change. Psychological Review, 84, 191-215.

https://www.brainyquote.com/quotes/authors/c/. charles_dickens.html

Brown, Brené. (2012). *Daring Greatly: How the Courage to be Vulnerable Transforms the Way We Live, Love, Parent, and Lead.* New York, NY: Gotham Books.

Brown, Brené and Whole-Heartedness

Cherry, K. A. (2005). Erikson's stages of psychosocial development. Retrieved from http://psychology.about.com/od/psychosocialtheories/a/psychosocial.htm

Dickens, Charles. Tale of Two Cities. Book 1: Recalled to life. Retrieved from http://literature.org/authors/dickens-charles/two-cities/book-01/chapter-01.html

Duckworth, A. L. (2013, April). The key to success? Grit. [Video file] Retrieved from (https://www.ted.com/talks/angela lee duckworth the key to success grit?language=en

Frankl, V. E. (1984). Man's search for meaning: An introduction to logotherapy.

Johnson, Sue. (2013). Love Sense: The Revolutionary New Science of Romantic Relationships. New York: Little, Brown and Company Hachette Book Group.

Kyne, P. B., & Axelrod, A. (2003). The go-getter: a story that tells you how to be one. Rev. ed. New York: Times Books.

McLeod, Saul. (2009). *Attachment Theory*. Retrieved from https://www.simplypsychology.org/attachment.html

Acknowledgements

To my dad, for being the first go-getter to inspire me; to my mom, for all the times she listened to me laying out my plans for my next Blue Vase; to Theresa Schopler.